DON'T BELIEVE EVERYTHING YOU THINK

Why Your Thinking is the Beginning & End of Suffering

ROBERT WARREN

TABLE OF CONTENT

INTRODUCTION

What if everything you've been taught about motivation and willpower is wrong? What if the key to overcoming anxiety, self-doubt, and self-sabotage lies not in pushing harder, but in thinking differently?

Welcome to "Don't Believe Everything You Think: Why Your Thinking Is the Beginning & End of Suffering."

This book is not just another self-help manual filled with generic advice. It's a revolutionary guide designed to take you on a transformative journey into the depths of your own mind. Here, you'll uncover the real reasons behind your psychological and emotional struggles, and learn practical, powerful strategies to break free from them.

Imagine a life where you are no longer at the mercy of your negative thoughts and limiting beliefs. A life where you embrace your true potential, guided by mindfulness, self-compassion, and inner wisdom. This book will show you how to make that life a reality.

In these pages, you'll discover:

- Why traditional concepts of motivation and willpower often fail us.
- How to identify and uproot the deep-seated causes of your suffering.
- Practical mindfulness techniques to ground yourself in the present moment.
- The transformative power of self-acceptance and compassion.
- Strategies to live a life driven by your true values and desires, rather than external validation.

"Don't Believe Everything You Think" is more than a book, it's your roadmap to mental freedom and personal transformation.
If you're ready to break free from the chains of your own mind and unlock a life of peace, joy, and fulfillment, then this book is for you.

Dive in, and discover how changing your thoughts can change your life.

THE AUTHOR - ROBERT WARREN

Robert Warren is a visionary author, speaker, and expert in the fields of mental health, personal development, and mindfulness. With a profound understanding of the human mind and its complexities, Robert has dedicated his career to helping individuals overcome psychological and emotional suffering and achieve lasting mental freedom.

With a background in psychology and extensive experience as a therapist, Robert brings a unique blend of professional expertise and personal insight to his work. He has spent years studying the intricacies of motivation, willpower, and the underlying factors that contribute to human suffering. His holistic approach integrates psychological techniques, mindfulness practices, and spiritual wisdom, providing readers with practical tools and transformative strategies for personal growth.

Robert is known for his compassionate and relatable writing style, which resonates deeply with readers. He has a remarkable ability to break down complex concepts into actionable steps, making it easier for individuals to implement positive changes in their lives. His work empowers people to challenge limiting beliefs, cultivate self-compassion, and embrace a life driven by their true values and desires.

As a sought-after speaker, Robert has delivered inspiring talks and workshops to diverse audiences, including corporate professionals, mental health practitioners, and individuals seeking personal transformation. His dynamic presentations and engaging storytelling have earned him a reputation as a thought leader in the field of personal development.

In addition to writing and speaking, Robert is passionate about ongoing learning and personal growth. He continues to explore new techniques and practices to enhance his own well-being and that of his readers. His dedication to helping others achieve mental freedom and a fulfilling life is evident in every aspect of his work.

Personal Life

When not writing or speaking, Robert enjoys hiking, meditating, and spending time with his family and pets, which help him stay grounded and connected to his own journey of self-discovery. He believes in the power of mindfulness, self-care, and continuous learning, values that he not only preaches but also practices in his daily life.

CHAPTER 1: RETHINKING MOTIVATION AND WILLPOWER

In the realm of overcoming psychological and emotional suffering, motivation and willpower have long been hailed as the champions of change. We have been led to believe that with enough motivation and willpower, we can conquer any obstacle, overcome any challenge, and achieve lasting transformation. But is this belief truly grounded in reality? In this chapter, we will delve into the illusion of motivation and willpower, exploring their limitations and unveiling a new paradigm for achieving mental freedom.

Motivation has often been seen as the internal drive that propels us towards our goals. It is intertwined with our desires, ambitions, and hopes for personal improvement. It is the force that pushes us forward, urging us to make positive changes in our lives. Similarly, willpower is regarded as the ability to persist and act in alignment with our motivation, even in the face of obstacles or difficulties.

While motivation and willpower may seem like the perfect recipe for success on the surface level, they often fall short when it comes to overcoming psychological and emotional suffering. The truth is that these struggles often have deeper roots that cannot be addressed solely through sheer determination or discipline. Distorted thought patterns, unresolved emotional trauma, and limiting beliefs can persist regardless of our level of motivation or determination.

Furthermore, prolonged emotional distress situations can easily deplete or compromise our willpower. When faced with intense stress or persistent difficulties, maintaining desired behaviors or overcoming harmful habits becomes an uphill battle even for individuals who are highly determined. And motivation itself can be influenced by external factors which are temporary at best; it can flicker out like a candle in the wind when faced with significant challenges.

So if motivation and willpower are not enough to bring about lasting change in our lives, what is? The new paradigm for achieving mental freedom lies in understanding the deeper causes of our suffering. It involves a comprehensive approach that integrates psychological techniques along with emotional and spiritual practices to effectively address psychological and emotional distress, promoting lasting inner transformation.

This approach may include techniques from cognitive-behavioral therapy to modify negative thought patterns, mindfulness to develop greater emotional awareness and resilience, and the practice of non-judgmental acceptance of emotions to promote emotional healing. By delving into the root causes of our suffering and embracing a more holistic approach, we can break free from the chains of reliance on motivation and willpower.

In this chapter, we will explore the common misconceptions surrounding motivation and willpower. We will debunk the belief that motivation is an infinite source of energy, highlighting its fluctuating nature and its dependence on external factors. We will also challenge the notion that willpower is a universal solution, emphasizing its limited capacity and susceptibility to depletion in the face of prolonged stress.

To shift our mindset away from relying solely on motivation and willpower, we must embark on a journey of self-discovery and inner transformation. This journey involves understanding the root causes of our suffering through introspection. It requires practicing mindfulness to cultivate present-moment awareness which allows us to observe our thoughts without judgment or attachment. It entails developing self-compassion by treating ourselves with kindness when faced with difficulties or setbacks.

Building sustainable habits plays an essential role in achieving lasting change as well. Instead of relying solely on motivation or sheer determination, we can focus on creating routines that support our goals while taking into account that there may be days when we lack motivation or feel depleted. By incorporating small steps towards progress into our daily lives, we can build momentum even during challenging times.

Developing our intuition is another crucial aspect of this new paradigm for achieving mental freedom. Intuition allows us to tap into our inner wisdom when making decisions or navigating through life's uncertainties. By honing this innate ability through practices such as meditation or journaling, we can gain clarity amidst chaos and trust ourselves more fully.

Utilizing psychological techniques can also be beneficial in our journey towards lasting change. Cognitive-behavioral therapy, for example, can help us identify and challenge negative thought patterns that contribute to our suffering. It provides us with practical tools to reframe our beliefs and adopt healthier perspectives.

In the chapters that follow, we will delve deeper into each of these aspects, unraveling the mysteries of the mind and guiding you towards a more profound understanding of yourself. Together, we will embark on a transformative journey, shedding the illusions of motivation and willpower and embracing a new paradigm for achieving lasting change.

So dear reader, let us embark on this path of self-discovery and liberation. Let us recognize that true change goes beyond mere motivation or willpower. By understanding the deeper causes of our suffering and integrating various techniques into our lives, we can break free from limiting beliefs and create a foundation for lasting transformation. The truth lies not in what we think but in what we choose to believe about ourselves and our capacity for growth.

CHAPTER 2: UNCOVERING THE UNDERLYING FACTORS OF SUFFERING

In this chapter, we embark on a journey to uncover the intricate web of causes that give rise to psychological and emotional suffering. We will delve into various aspects such as distorted thought patterns, limiting beliefs, unresolved emotional trauma, chronic stress, environmental and social factors, biological and genetic influences, lack of purpose or meaning in life, emotional dysregulation, and cultural and societal pressures. By gaining a deeper understanding of these root causes, we can begin to identify and address the underlying issues that impact our mental well-being.

Distorted thought patterns have a profound impact on how we perceive reality and shape our emotions. For instance, catastrophizing - magnifying the negative aspects of situations - creates a vicious cycle of pessimism and despair. Similarly, black-and-white thinking limits our ability to see shades of gray in life's complexities. These distorted thought patterns contribute to chronic stress and anxiety that lead to psychological distress.

Limiting beliefs are deeply ingrained notions about ourselves and the world around us that significantly influence our emotional well-being. Beliefs such as "I am not good enough" or "People cannot be trusted" restrict our personal growth and happiness. These self-imposed limitations hinder us from reaching our full potential unless we challenge them head-on.

Unresolved emotional trauma is another factor that contributes to suffering. Whether stemming from childhood experiences or later in life, unprocessed trauma leaves lasting scars that can manifest as anxiety disorders like PTSD or depression if left unaddressed.

Chronic stress is caused by prolonged exposure to stressors that overwhelm our coping mechanisms. It leads to burnout and emotional exhaustion when we continuously struggle without respite or support.

Environmental factors play a significant role in our psychological well-being. Toxic work environments drain us emotionally while dysfunctional relationships erode our sense of self-worth. Societal pressures impose unrealistic standards upon us which contribute to feelings of inadequacy.

Lack of purpose or meaning in life can result in a profound sense of emptiness and depression. Without a clear sense of direction and fulfillment, we may find ourselves adrift, searching for something meaningful to anchor our lives.

Emotional dysregulation refers to the difficulty in managing and regulating emotions. This can lead to mood disorders and instability that further contribute to our suffering.

Cultural and societal influences impose norms, values, and expectations upon us that shape our beliefs and behaviors. Rigid gender roles, idealized images portrayed in media and social platforms, as well as the desire to fit in with peers can all contribute to psychological distress.

Biological and genetic factors also play a role in our emotional well-being. Chemical imbalances in the brain, genetic predispositions, or physical health problems can all impact how we experience suffering.

Understanding these root causes allows us to identify the underlying issues affecting our mental health. It provides us with an opportunity for self-reflection and growth as we seek ways to alleviate our suffering.

To address these causes effectively, it is crucial that we challenge and reframe distorted thought patterns and limiting beliefs. Through self-reflection exercises like journaling or mindfulness practices, we become aware of these patterns and beliefs. By questioning their validity and examining evidence for or against them, we can begin the process of cognitive restructuring. This involves reframing negative thoughts into more balanced ones that align with reality rather than perpetuating harmful narratives about ourselves or the world around us.

Gradually exposing ourselves to situations that challenge our limiting beliefs also plays a pivotal role in lasting change. Reinforcing positive behaviors strengthens new neural pathways while weakening old ones associated with suffering.

Childhood experiences have a profound impact on shaping thought patterns and behaviors that contribute to suffering later in life. Positive early relationships with caregivers foster secure attachment styles while negative experiences can result in insecure attachment styles leading to difficulties forming healthy relationships later on. Trauma and abuse during childhood can leave lasting effects, resulting in fears, trust issues, and a sense of worthlessness. Parental influence and societal norms also shape our beliefs and behaviors. Rigid gender roles, idealized images portrayed in media and social platforms, as well as the desire to fit in with peers can all contribute to psychological distress.

Practical steps that readers can take to identify and address the root causes of their own suffering include self-reflection and awareness through journaling or mindfulness practices. Identifying negative thought patterns and beliefs through thought records allows us to challenge them by questioning their validity. This process leads to a more realistic and balanced perspective. Exploring childhood experiences through life timelines or inner child work provides insight into how these experiences influence our present emotions and actions.

Therapeutic techniques such as cognitive-behavioral therapy (CBT) or acceptance and commitment therapy (ACT) offer structured support in addressing deep-rooted issues. These approaches provide tools for challenging negative thought patterns, building resilience, developing healthy coping mechanisms, embracing self-compassion, cultivating positive mindsets, practicing gratitude, affirmations, among other techniques that contribute to overall well-being.

Building a support network is crucial as well - whether it's seeking professional help or joining support groups - it provides a sense of community where shared experiences foster understanding and growth.

By understanding the root causes of our suffering and actively working towards addressing them using practical strategies like those outlined above - we pave the way for more effective healing that is both transformative and lasting.

In the next chapter, we will explore the power of self-compassion on our journey towards overcoming suffering. We will examine how this fundamental practice allows us to cultivate kindness towards ourselves while fostering resilience in the face of adversity. Through self-compassion, we learn to embrace our imperfections with love rather than judgment - leading us towards greater emotional well-being.

CHAPTER 3: CULTIVATING MINDFULNESS AND AWARENESS

In our fast-paced and often chaotic lives, it can be easy to get caught up in the whirlwind of our thoughts and emotions. We find ourselves reacting automatically, without pausing to consider the impact of our actions. But what if there was a way to break free from this cycle? What if we could cultivate a sense of mindfulness and awareness that would allow us to observe our thoughts and emotions without becoming overwhelmed by them?

Present-moment awareness, often cultivated through mindfulness practices, is crucial in reducing the impact of thoughts and emotions. It offers a multitude of benefits that can transform our lives. Let's explore some of these benefits and discover how we can incorporate mindfulness and awareness into our daily lives.

One of the key advantages of present-moment awareness is the reduction of automatic reactions. When we are aware of the present moment, we can observe our thoughts and emotions as they arise, rather than reacting automatically. This awareness creates a space between stimulus and response, allowing for more thoughtful and intentional reactions rather than knee-jerk responses. It empowers us to choose how we want to respond to a situation, rather than being driven by our emotions.

Furthermore, present-moment awareness helps us decrease our identification with thoughts and emotions. Mindfulness encourages us to take an observer stance towards our thoughts and emotions, seeing them as transient mental events rather than defining aspects of our identity. This reduces the tendency to become entangled with negative thoughts and emotions, diminishing their power to cause distress. We can learn to observe our thoughts and emotions without judgment, allowing them to come and go without getting caught up in their content.

Emotional regulation is another area where present-moment awareness shines. By being mindful of the present moment, we can accurately recognize and label our emotions, which is the first step in effective emotional regulation. This leads to reduced intensity and duration of negative emotional states, improving our overall emotional well-being. We become more attuned to our emotions and can respond to them in a healthier and more balanced way.

Rumination and worry are common challenges that many of us face. Mindfulness shifts our focus from past regrets and future worries to the present moment. Rumination and worry are often about things that have already happened or might happen, not what is happening now. By focusing on the present, we can break the cycle of rumination and worry, which are major contributors to anxiety and depression. We learn to anchor ourselves in the present moment, finding peace and clarity.

Cognitive flexibility is another gift that present-moment awareness bestows upon us. It fosters an open-minded and flexible approach to experiences. Mindfulness encourages us to see things as they are, without preconceived notions or judgments. This cognitive flexibility helps us adapt to new information and changing circumstances, reducing the stress associated with rigidity in thinking. We become more open to different perspectives and possibilities, expanding our horizons and enriching our lives.

Stress management is a significant aspect of our well-being, and present-moment awareness plays a vital role in this area. Being mindful of the present moment reduces the physiological and psychological impact of stress by preventing the mind from dwelling on stressors beyond the current moment. This reduction in perceived stress can lower overall stress levels, contributing to better mental and physical health. We learn to navigate through life's challenges with greater resilience and grace.

Self-compassion is another beautiful byproduct of present-moment awareness. When we practice mindfulness, we often include elements of self-compassion, treating ourselves with the same kindness and understanding we would offer a friend. This helps mitigate the harsh self-criticism that can accompany negative thoughts and emotions, leading to a more balanced and gentle approach to personal challenges. We learn to be our own best friend, offering ourselves love and support.

Acceptance is a fundamental aspect of mindfulness. It promotes the acceptance of thoughts and emotions as they are, without trying to change or resist them. This does not mean resignation, but rather acknowledging their presence without added judgment or struggle. Acceptance reduces the additional layer of suffering created by resisting or fighting against unpleasant thoughts and emotions, making them easier to manage. We learn to embrace the present moment, with all its imperfections and uncertainties.

Enhanced focus and concentration are additional benefits of present-moment awareness. Practicing mindfulness improves attention control and concentration, helping us stay focused on the task at hand. Improved concentration can reduce the mental clutter caused by intrusive thoughts and emotions, leading to greater productivity and mental clarity. We become more present and engaged in our daily activities, enhancing our overall effectiveness.

Now that we understand the importance and benefits of cultivating mindfulness and awareness, let's explore some practical techniques and practices that can help us integrate these qualities into our daily lives.

One of the most well-known practices for cultivating mindfulness is mindfulness meditation. By setting aside dedicated time each day to sit quietly and focus on our breath or bodily sensations, we can strengthen our ability to be present. During meditation, we may notice our mind wandering, but the key is to gently bring our attention back to our breath without judgment. This practice builds our capacity to observe our thoughts and emotions without becoming overwhelmed by them.

Another technique is mindful breathing. Taking a few moments throughout the day to focus solely on our breathing can anchor us in the present moment. We observe the inhale and exhale, counting each breath cycle up to ten and then starting again. This simple practice can be done anywhere, anytime, and helps us stay connected to the present moment.

Mindful observation is another powerful technique. We can pause and take a moment to observe our surroundings using each of our five senses. This exercise grounds us in the present by heightening our sensory awareness. We identify five things we can see, four things we can touch, three things we can hear, two things we can smell, and one thing we can taste. This practice helps us fully engage with the present moment and appreciate the richness of our sensory experiences.

Mindful eating is a practice that encourages us to focus entirely on the act of eating. During meals, we pay attention to the flavors, textures, and aromas of our food. We chew slowly and thoroughly, savoring each bite and noticing the process of tasting and swallowing. By avoiding distractions like TV or smartphones, we can fully immerse ourselves in the present moment and cultivate a deeper connection with our food.

Mindful movement practices, such as yoga, Tai Chi, or Qigong, are excellent ways to integrate mindfulness into our bodies. As we engage in these practices, we pay attention to the sensations in our bodies, maintaining awareness of our breath. We become fully present in the movements, connecting mind and body in a harmonious dance. These practices not only enhance our physical well-being but also cultivate mindfulness and awareness.

Incorporating mindfulness into our daily routines can be a powerful way to anchor ourselves in the present moment. We can start our day with a few minutes of mindfulness, such as a short meditation, mindful stretching, or focused breathing. Setting an intention for the day to remain present and aware can set the tone for a mindful and fulfilling day.

Throughout the day, we can use reminders to bring our attention back to the present moment. Whether it's a phone alarm, a sticky note, or a bracelet, these reminders serve as gentle nudges to pause, take a few deep breaths, and notice our current thoughts and sensations.

Journaling is another valuable tool for cultivating mindfulness and awareness. Keeping a mindfulness journal allows us to write about our experiences, thoughts, and feelings. We can reflect on moments of awareness throughout the day and recognize patterns that arise. This practice deepens our understanding of our own minds and supports our mindfulness journey.

Gratitude is a powerful practice that shifts our focus from negative to positive aspects of life. By writing down three things we are grateful for each day, we cultivate a more mindful and appreciative mindset. This practice enhances our overall well-being and helps us find joy in the present moment.

Mindful listening and communication are essential skills that can transform our relationships and interactions with others. By practicing active listening, we can focus entirely on the speaker without planning our response. This deepens our connection with others and fosters more meaningful conversations. Mindful communication involves speaking with intention and kindness, considering the impact of our words on others. We become more present and attuned to the needs of those around us.

As we embark on the journey of cultivating mindfulness and awareness, we may encounter various challenges and obstacles. Restlessness and impatience can make it difficult for us to sit still and focus on the present moment. To overcome this, we can start small and gradually increase the duration of our mindfulness sessions. Engaging in movement-based practices, such as mindful walking or yoga, can also help restlessness individuals incorporate mindfulness into their lives.

Intrusive thoughts and emotions can be another challenge during mindfulness practice. We may find our minds flooded with thoughts, making it hard to stay focused. To overcome this, we can practice labeling thoughts and emotions as they arise, acknowledging them without getting caught up in their content. Guided meditations can also provide structure and support, helping us maintain focus during our mindfulness practice.

Self-criticism and judgment can hinder our progress in cultivating mindfulness and awareness. We may judge ourselves for not "doing it right" or for having a busy mind during practice. To overcome this, we can cultivate self-compassion and recognize that mindfulness is a practice. There is no "perfect" way to practice mindfulness; it's about the effort and intention rather than the outcome.

Boredom can also be a challenge when it comes to mindfulness. Our minds may perceive mindfulness as boring or uninteresting, especially in a world filled with constant stimulation. To overcome this, we can incorporate variety into our practice by trying different mindfulness techniques. Approaching each session with curiosity can also help us stay engaged and open to the experience.

Time constraints are a common obstacle when it comes to mindfulness practice. Finding time in our busy schedules can be challenging. To overcome this, we can integrate mindfulness into our daily routines. We can practice mindfulness during everyday activities, such as brushing our teeth, eating, or commuting. We can also utilize short mindfulness practices, such as a few deep breaths or a one-minute body scan, throughout the day.

Doubt and skepticism may arise when we first start practicing mindfulness. We may question its effectiveness or feel skeptical about its benefits. To overcome this, we can educate ourselves about the science and benefits of mindfulness. Reading books, articles, or taking courses can build our understanding and confidence. We can also commit to trying mindfulness for a set period to experience its effects firsthand before making a judgment.

Emotional discomfort can be another challenge on our mindfulness journey. Mindfulness can bring up uncomfortable emotions that we may prefer to avoid. To overcome this, we can practice gradual exposure, starting with practices that feel safe and manageable and gradually increasing exposure to more challenging emotions. Creating a supportive environment, possibly with the guidance of a therapist or mindfulness teacher, can also be helpful.

Lack of immediate results can discourage us from continuing our mindfulness practice. We may expect instant benefits and become disheartened when we don't see them. To overcome this, we can practice patience and persistence. Mindfulness is a gradual process that requires consistent practice over time. We can also celebrate small wins, acknowledging and appreciating the small improvements and moments of mindfulness along the way.

Physical discomfort, such as sitting for extended periods, can be a challenge during mindfulness practice. To overcome this, we can find a comfortable posture that supports our body, whether it's sitting on a chair, using cushions, or lying down. Incorporating mindful movement, such as stretching or gentle movement, before or after sitting practices can also alleviate discomfort.

Distractions are another common obstacle when it comes to mindfulness practice. External distractions, such as noise, interruptions, or a busy environment, can disrupt our focus. To overcome this, we can create a supportive environment by finding a quiet space or using noise-canceling headphones. We can also practice letting go of distractions and gently redirecting our attention back to the present moment.

By cultivating mindfulness and awareness, we can overcome anxiety, self-doubt, and self-sabotage. Let's explore some real-life examples of how these practices have helped individuals transform their lives.

Sarah, a marketing executive, struggled with chronic anxiety that affected her work performance and personal life. Through mindfulness meditation and mindful breathing, she learned to detach from her anxious thoughts and reduce the frequency and intensity of her anxiety episodes. She became more focused and productive at work, and her overall emotional well-being improved.

James, a software developer, constantly doubted his abilities despite being successful in his career. Through mindfulness practices and gratitude journaling, he learned to observe his self-doubting thoughts without getting entangled in them. He began to see these thoughts as temporary and not reflective of his true abilities. His self-confidence grew, leading to better performance and recognition from his peers.

Emma, a freelance writer, had a pattern of procrastinating on important projects, leading to missed deadlines and financial instability. Through mindfulness practices, such as mindful eating and mindful walking, she became more aware of her procrastination triggers and learned to make more productive choices. She experienced increased productivity and a sense of fulfillment in her work.

John, a teacher, experienced intense social anxiety that made it difficult for him to interact with colleagues and students. Through mindfulness-based stress reduction and mindfulness group sessions, he learned to observe his anxious thoughts and bodily sensations without judgment. This reduced his overall anxiety and improved his social skills, leading to stronger relationships and a more fulfilling professional life.

Laura, a graphic designer, struggled with perfectionism, which led to constant self-criticism and burnout. Through mindful self-compassion and loving-kindness meditation, she learned to treat herself with kindness and understanding. She shifted her focus from perfectionism to a more balanced approach to her work, recognizing that mistakes are part of the learning process. She experienced improved well-being and a greater sense of inner peace.

These real-life examples illustrate the transformative power of mindfulness and awareness. By cultivating these qualities, we can overcome anxiety, self-doubt, and self-sabotage, leading to a more fulfilled and balanced life.

Cultivating mindfulness and awareness is a powerful practice that can bring about profound changes in our lives. It allows us to observe our thoughts and emotions without becoming overwhelmed by them, leading to greater emotional stability, resilience, and self-compassion. By staying present in the moment, we can reduce stress, enhance our focus and concentration, and develop a deeper connection with ourselves and others. As we navigate the challenges and obstacles on this journey, let us remember that mindfulness is a practice, and every moment is an opportunity to cultivate awareness and find freedom in our minds.

CHAPTER 4: TAPPING INTO INNER WISDOM AND INTUITION

Michael, a high-powered executive in his fifties, was constantly under immense pressure and experienced chronic stress. The demands of his job seemed never-ending, and he often found himself overwhelmed by the weight of responsibility on his shoulders. Seeking relief from this constant state of tension, Michael embarked on a journey of self-discovery and personal growth.

He had heard about the benefits of meditation and mindfulness practices and decided to give them a try. With an open mind and a willingness to explore new avenues for finding inner peace, Michael began incorporating daily meditation sessions into his routine. He set aside time each morning to sit quietly, focusing on his breath and allowing any thoughts or emotions that arose to simply pass through him without judgment.

At first, it was challenging for Michael to quiet his busy mind. Thoughts would come rushing in – deadlines at work, upcoming meetings, personal obligations – threatening to derail his attempts at finding stillness. But with consistent practice and gentle persistence, he began to notice a shift in his experience.

Through these regular meditation sessions, Michael started developing a heightened sense of awareness. He became more attuned to the present moment – the feeling of cool air against his skin as he breathed in deeply; the sound of birds chirping outside his window; the warmth of sunlight streaming through the curtains. These small moments became anchors for him amidst the chaos of daily life.

As he continued with this practice, Michael also noticed something else: an increased ability to observe his own thoughts and emotions without becoming entangled in them. In moments where stress threatened to overwhelm him –

during heated meetings or when faced with tight deadlines – he would take a step back mentally and observe what was happening within himself.

This newfound clarity allowed Michael to respond rather than react impulsively. Instead of lashing out or shutting down when faced with difficult situations at work or home, he would take a deep breath and consider alternative perspectives before proceeding. This pause gave him the opportunity to make more conscious choices, aligning his actions with his values and long-term goals.

As he deepened his practice, Michael also began incorporating mindfulness exercises into his daily life. Instead of rushing from one task to another, he started paying attention to each moment as it unfolded. Whether it was savoring a cup of tea in the morning or fully engaging in a conversation with a colleague, Michael made an effort to be fully present.

This shift in mindset had a profound impact on Michael's well-being. Not only did he experience a reduction in stress levels, but he also noticed improvements in other areas of his life. His relationships with colleagues and loved ones became more authentic and meaningful as he cultivated the ability to truly listen and connect with others. He became more attuned to his own needs and priorities, making self-care a non-negotiable part of his routine.

The transformative power of tapping into inner wisdom and intuition became evident not only in Michael's life but also in the lives of others who had embarked on similar journeys. Through mindfulness, meditation, and other practices, these individuals were able to overcome anxiety, self-doubt, self-sabotage, and other challenges that had previously held them back.

Sarah, a young mother struggling with postpartum depression found solace in meditation. By creating space for herself each day to sit quietly and observe her thoughts without judgment or attachment, she was able to develop greater self-compassion and find joy in even the simplest moments with her child.

David, an entrepreneur facing immense pressure to succeed at all costs learned how mindfulness could help him navigate challenging situations without sacrificing his well-being or compromising his values. By observing his thoughts before taking action or making decisions under duress, he discovered that there was often a wiser course of action that took into account both short-term demands and long-term consequences.

These personal stories serve as inspiration for anyone seeking to cultivate inner peace and personal growth. They are a testament to the power of connecting with our inner wisdom, which can guide us through life's ups and downs with grace and resilience.

In a world that often values external achievements above all else, these practices remind us that true success comes from within. By making space for stillness, mindfulness, and self-reflection, we can tap into our own innate wisdom and intuition. This allows us to navigate life's challenges with greater clarity and purpose, ultimately leading to a more fulfilled and meaningful existence.

So whether you're a high-powered executive like Michael or someone grappling with the everyday stresses of life, consider incorporating meditation and mindfulness practices into your routine. Start small – just a few minutes each day – and gradually build up from there. Notice how these moments of stillness begin to ripple outwards, positively influencing all aspects of your life.

Remember that this is not about achieving perfection or instant results. It's about embracing the process of self-discovery and personal growth. Be patient with yourself as you embark on this journey. Celebrate even the smallest victories along the way.

As Michael discovered firsthand, the rewards are immeasurable. Cultivating inner calm, presence, and self-awareness can lead to profound transformations in all areas of our lives – from our relationships to our work to our overall well-being.

So take a deep breath, close your eyes if it feels right for you, and begin your own exploration of meditation and mindfulness today. Your inner wisdom is waiting to be discovered – embrace it wholeheartedly on this beautiful journey towards self-discovery.

CHAPTER 5: LETTING GO OF THOUGHTS TO FIND INNER PEACE

In today's fast-paced world, our thoughts have the power to consume us. They can easily spiral into negativity and limit our potential for happiness and well-being. Recognizing the transient nature of thoughts and detaching from negative or limiting ones is a practice that has been emphasized in mindfulness and cognitive-behavioral therapies. This practice can significantly improve our mental health and overall well-being. In this chapter, we will explore why letting go of attachment to thoughts is so important, as well as practical techniques for cultivating non-attachment.

To fully understand the significance of non-attachment to thoughts, it is essential to first grasp the nature of thoughts themselves. Thoughts are not permanent fixtures in our minds; rather, they are fleeting mental events. They arise, exist for a while, and eventually dissipate. By recognizing this transient nature, we can avoid getting stuck in a cycle of negative thinking. Just because a thought occurs does not mean it is true or reflective of reality. Negative or limiting thoughts often distort or exaggerate actual circumstances. Understanding this helps us not take every thought at face value.

Detaching from negative or limiting thoughts brings about numerous benefits that positively impact our emotional well-being. It reduces emotional distress by allowing us to observe our thoughts without becoming overwhelmed by them. This detachment enables better emotional regulation since we can choose how to respond to distressing thoughts instead of reacting impulsively. Moreover, detaching from negative thoughts promotes mental clarity by clearing away the clutter caused by constant rumination over negativity.

This leads to improved focus and decision-making abilities in various aspects of life. Most importantly, cultivating non-attachment creates space for more constructive thoughts and encourages positive thinking which enhances mood, motivation, and overall mental health.

Now that we understand why non-attachment is crucial let's explore practical techniques that can help us cultivate this mindset towards our own thoughts:

1. Mindfulness Meditation: Mindfulness meditation is a powerful tool for observing thoughts as they arise and pass away. By practicing mindfulness, we reinforce the idea that thoughts are transient and not inherently tied to reality. This allows us to develop a sense of detachment from our thoughts, viewing them from a place of observation rather than becoming entangled in them.

2. Cognitive Restructuring: Cognitive-behavioral techniques, such as cognitive restructuring, can help us challenge and reframe negative thoughts. By questioning the validity of our negative thoughts and finding evidence against them, we can actively reshape our thinking patterns. This process helps us detach from negative or limiting thoughts by recognizing their inaccuracies or distortions.

3. Journaling: Another effective technique for cultivating non-attachment is journaling. By externalizing our thoughts onto paper, we gain perspective on them and recognize any recurring patterns or themes that may be holding us back. Journaling also provides us with an opportunity to reflect on our emotions and gain insights into how certain thoughts may be affecting our well-being.

4. Labeling Thoughts: Labeling our thoughts is a simple yet powerful method for creating distance between ourselves and the content of our minds. By consciously labeling a thought as just a thought instead of identifying with it, we reduce its emotional impact on us. This practice helps us detach from negative or limiting thoughts more easily.

5. Body Awareness Practices: Engaging in body awareness practices like yoga or Tai Chi can promote relaxation and detachment from unhelpful thoughts. These practices bring our focus to the present moment, allowing us to let go of mental chatter and become more attuned to sensations in the body.

6. Practicing Gratitude: Cultivating gratitude is an effective way to counterbalance negative thinking patterns with more positive ones. When we intentionally focus on what we are grateful for, it becomes easier to see negative thoughts as transient experiences that do not define who we are. This shift in perspective helps us detach from negative thoughts and reduces their significance in our lives.

The psychological and emotional benefits of non-attachment to thoughts are vast. By reducing cognitive distortions, we build resilience and can bounce back from negative experiences and thoughts more quickly. Furthermore, cultivating non-attachment enhances our relationships by improving emotional regulation and mental clarity. When we detach from negative or limiting thoughts, we become more effective communicators and gain a greater capacity for empathy towards others. Moreover, non-attachment fosters self-compassion by recognizing that negative thoughts do not define our true selves. This recognition encourages a kinder, more compassionate approach to ourselves.

To illustrate the transformative power of letting go of attachment to thoughts, let's explore some real-life examples:

1. *Emily struggled with anxiety for many years.* Through mindfulness meditation, she learned to observe her anxious thoughts without getting caught up in them. This practice brought her calmness and presence in the face of anxiety-inducing situations.

2. *Mark had a habit of being overly self-critical, which hindered his self-confidence and personal growth.* By practicing cognitive restructuring techniques, he was able to challenge his negative thoughts and reframe them into more empowering beliefs about himself. This newfound perspective allowed him to overcome self-criticism and gain self-confidence.

3. *Lisa was a perfectionist who often felt overwhelmed by her own expectations.* Through mindfulness meditation and cultivating self-compassion, she discovered joy in imperfection and learned to embrace herself as she was rather than constantly striving for an unattainable ideal.

4. *John struggled with social anxiety that made it difficult for him to connect with others on a deeper level.* Through mindfulness-based stress reduction practices, he found inner peace by learning to let go of worries about what others thought of him or how he might be perceived socially.

5. Anna had experienced past trauma that continued to haunt her through intrusive thoughts and negative self-beliefs. Through mindfulness and acceptance practices, she was able to heal from her trauma and cultivate self-love. By letting go of attachment to her traumatic thoughts, she found freedom and a sense of peace within herself.

6. David had a high-stress job that often left him feeling overwhelmed and exhausted. By practicing mindfulness techniques, he learned to let go of negative thoughts related to work stress and redirect his focus to the present moment. This shift in mindset improved his overall well-being and allowed him to find joy even amidst challenging circumstances.

Non-attachment to thoughts is a transformative practice that can bring immense benefits to our mental health and overall well-being. By recognizing the transient nature of thoughts and detaching from negative or limiting ones, we can find inner peace, joy, and freedom in our lives. So let us embark on this journey of non-attachment together and discover the profound impact it can have on our well-being.

CHAPTER 6: THE TRANSFORMATIVE POWER OF ACCEPTANCE AND COMPASSION

In the journey of overcoming anxiety, self-doubt, and self-sabotage, practicing self-acceptance and compassion towards oneself and others plays a significant role. These practices not only foster a healthier relationship with oneself but also enhance emotional resilience, leading to greater overall well-being. In this chapter, we will explore why acceptance and compassion are so significant in this transformative process.

Self-acceptance is a crucial component in managing and reducing anxiety. When individuals accept themselves as they are, without harsh judgment or unrealistic expectations, they create a mental space where anxiety is less likely to thrive. By embracing one's flaws and imperfections as part of their unique journey, the fear of failure and the pressure to meet unattainable standards diminish significantly. For example, let's consider Sarah's story. She often felt anxious about her performance at work, constantly worrying about making mistakes or not meeting expectations. However, when she started practicing self-compassion by acknowledging her efforts and accepting that it's okay to make mistakes sometimes, she experienced a shift in mindset that reduced her anxiety levels drastically. This newfound perspective allowed her to approach her tasks with more confidence and calmness.

Similarly, self-doubt often stems from a harsh inner critic that constantly questions one's abilities and worthiness. However, by practicing self-compassion, individuals learn to treat themselves with kindness and understanding – just as they would treat a friend in a similar situation. This change in perspective can significantly reduce self-doubt over time.

Take Mark's example: he was a software developer who doubted his skills despite receiving positive feedback from colleagues and clients alike. However, when he incorporated self-compassion techniques into his life – such as acknowledging his achievements and offering himself encouragement instead of criticism – he gradually built up his confidence levels while diminishing his self-doubt.

Self-sabotage occurs when individuals undermine their own goals and success due to deep-seated feelings of unworthiness or fear of failure. The practice of self-acceptance helps break this destructive cycle by fostering a sense of worthiness and self-respect. When individuals fully accept themselves as they are, including their imperfections, they are more likely to pursue their goals without the constant fear of failure or the need for perfection. Let's consider Emma's story: she was a writer who often procrastinated and missed deadlines due to her self-sabotaging behaviors rooted in a fear of not being good enough. However, once she started practicing self-acceptance by embracing her imperfections and taking consistent steps towards her goals, she gradually overcame her self-sabotaging tendencies, ultimately achieving greater success.

Moreover, extending compassion towards others also plays a vital role in building healthier relationships and social connections. By cultivating compassion for others, individuals can improve their empathy and reduce conflicts, creating a supportive social environment. This positive social support can further help in managing anxiety and self-doubt. Consider John's experience: he struggled with social anxiety and often felt overwhelmed in social situations. However, when he actively practiced compassion by focusing on understanding and empathizing with others' perspectives instead of solely worrying about his own insecurities, he started feeling more connected to those around him while experiencing less anxiety.

The practice of self-acceptance and compassion leads to greater emotional resilience – the ability to bounce back from setbacks and challenges without becoming overwhelmed or defeated. When individuals are kind to themselves through self-compassion practices, they develop the inner strength necessary to handle life's ups and downs with grace. This resilience is crucial in overcoming anxiety, self-doubt, and self-sabotage effectively. Let's consider Laura's story: she faced intense self-criticism due to her perfectionistic tendencies that left no room for mistakes or failures. However, when she started practicing self-compassion and learning to accept herself and her imperfections as a natural part of being human, she developed the resilience needed to handle criticism and failures more constructively. This newfound resilience led to a more balanced and fulfilling life.

In summary, self-acceptance and compassion are powerful tools in overcoming anxiety, self-doubt, and self-sabotage. These practices not only help individuals build a positive relationship with themselves but also foster emotional resilience that allows them to navigate life's challenges with greater ease. Moreover, extending compassion towards others creates a supportive social environment that enhances overall well-being. By embracing self-acceptance and compassion, individuals can experience a profound transformation – finding inner peace, joy, and an empowered sense of self that positively impacts every aspect of their lives. So take the first step today – practice acceptance and compassion towards yourself and others – and witness the transformative power it holds for your journey towards personal growth and fulfillment.

CHAPTER 7: EMBRACING INNER FREEDOM AND SELF-DETERMINATION

In this chapter, we will explore the concept of moving away from relying on external forces and fostering inner freedom and self-determination. This shift involves developing the ability to make choices and take actions based on one's inner values, beliefs, and desires, rather than being driven by external validation or societal expectations.

Inner Freedom refers to the state of being free from internal and external constraints that limit one's ability to think, feel, and act authentically. It involves being true to oneself and not being overly influenced by external pressures or opinions. Self-Determination, on the other hand, is the ability to control one's own life and make decisions independently. It involves taking responsibility for one's actions and outcomes, setting personal goals, and working towards them with a sense of purpose and direction.

To move away from relying on external forces, individuals need to shift their focus from seeking validation and approval from others to finding strength and guidance within themselves. This shift involves several key practices:

1. Developing Self-Awareness: Cultivating a deep understanding of one's values, beliefs, and desires is essential for inner freedom. By becoming more self-aware, individuals can recognize what truly matters to them separate from societal expectations or external influences.

2. Embracing Authenticity: Being authentic means expressing oneself honestly and living in alignment with one's true values and beliefs. By prioritizing authenticity in their lives, individuals can make choices that resonate with their true selves rather than seeking approval or avoiding criticism.

3. Building Self-Confidence: Developing self-confidence is crucial for fostering inner freedom. Building self-confidence involves setting personal goals that align with one's values; acknowledging accomplishments; practicing self-compassion; celebrating small wins along the way; surrounding oneself with supportive people who uplift them; taking risks outside of their comfort zone; recognizing that mistakes are opportunities for growth.

4. Setting Personal Boundaries: Establishing and maintaining healthy boundaries helps individuals protect their inner freedom and autonomy. Boundaries define what is acceptable and unacceptable in relationships and interactions, allowing individuals to prioritize their well-being and values. Setting personal boundaries involves recognizing one's limits, communicating assertively, saying no when needed, and valuing one's needs without feeling guilty.

5. Cultivating Internal Motivation: Focusing on intrinsic motivation, driven by internal desires and satisfaction rather than extrinsic motivation, fosters self-determination. Pursuing activities and goals that are personally meaningful encourages a sense of purpose and autonomy. Cultivating internal motivation involves identifying one's passions; setting meaningful goals aligned with those passions; breaking down larger goals into smaller achievable steps; finding joy in the process rather than solely focusing on the outcome; seeking inspiration from within rather than relying on external validation.

To foster inner freedom and self-determination, individuals can engage in practices that reinforce their autonomy and inner strength:

1. Mindfulness: Practicing mindfulness allows individuals to stay connected to their inner experiences while reducing the influence of external distractions. By being fully present in each moment, individuals can make conscious choices that align with their true selves.

2. Meditation: Regular meditation practice helps quiet the mind, increase self-awareness, reduce stress levels, enhance focus, improve emotional well-being, cultivate compassion towards oneself and others.

3. Goal Setting: Setting clear personal goals provides a roadmap for progress toward fulfilling one's aspirations. By breaking down larger goals into smaller manageable tasks or milestones along the way helps maintain motivation as they experience a sense of progress.

4. Planning: Developing a strategic plan for achieving personal goals ensures focused effort towards desired outcomes while managing time effectively through prioritization.

5. Intrinsic Motivation: Understanding intrinsic motivation is key to fostering self-determination as it involves doing something because it is inherently interesting or enjoyable instead of relying solely on willpower or external rewards. Individuals can develop intrinsic motivation by identifying their personal values and interests and setting meaningful goals that align with them. Finding enjoyment in the process, cultivating curiosity, and celebrating small wins are also effective strategies for fostering intrinsic motivation.

6. Self-Discipline: Building self-discipline helps individuals stay committed to their goals even when faced with challenges or distractions. It involves creating a routine, setting clear boundaries, practicing delayed gratification, using positive self-talk and affirmations, holding oneself accountable for actions and decisions.

While individuals may face barriers and obstacles when trying to free themselves from dependence on willpower and motivation, there are strategies to overcome them:

1. *Lack of Clear Goals*: Setting specific, measurable, achievable, relevant, and time-bound (SMART) goals helps clarify one's direction and purpose.

2. *Overwhelming Tasks:* Breaking down overwhelming tasks or goals into smaller manageable steps prevents procrastination by making the process more approachable.

3. *Inconsistent Routines*: Establishing consistent routines provides structure and helps individuals stay focused on their priorities.

4. External Distractions: Minimizing external distractions such as turning off notifications on electronic devices or creating a dedicated workspace can enhance focus and productivity.

5. Negative Self-Talk: Practicing positive self-talk involves replacing negative thoughts with positive affirmations that reinforce one's abilities and strengths.

6. Lack of Immediate Rewards: Recognizing that progress takes time allows individuals to find satisfaction in the process itself rather than relying solely on immediate rewards or external validation.

7. Unrealistic Expectations: Setting realistic expectations ensures that individuals do not become discouraged by setting unattainable standards for themselves.

8. Dependence on External Validation: Shifting the focus from seeking validation from others to finding validation within oneself promotes inner freedom and autonomy.

9. Lack of Social Support: Surrounding oneself with supportive individuals who uplift them can provide encouragement during challenging times; seeking out community groups or support networks that share similar goals or interests.

Several examples illustrate how individuals have successfully embraced inner freedom and self-determination to create fulfilling lives:

1. Maria's Career Transformation: Maria felt unfulfilled in her previous career, which did not align with her passions and values. By transitioning into a career that resonated with her authentic self, Maria found fulfillment and happiness. She took the time to explore her interests, reflect on her values, and make a plan for pursuing a new path.

2. Tom's Health and Wellness Journey: Tom realized that he needed to prioritize his health and well-being but struggled with consistency in his efforts. By embracing intrinsic motivation and self-discipline, he made choices that aligned with his interests such as engaging in physical activities he enjoyed rather than forcing himself into traditional exercise routines. Over time, Tom achieved a healthier lifestyle without solely relying on willpower.

3. Emily's Artistic Pursuit: Emily had always been passionate about art but never pursued it seriously due to societal expectations of pursuing more "practical" careers. However, she eventually decided to embrace her true passion by enrolling in art classes and dedicating time each day to practice her craft diligently despite facing challenges along the way. Through authenticity and perseverance, Emily created a fulfilling career that resonated with her true self.

4. David's Lifelong Learning: David believed in continuous self-improvement and personal growth but had previously felt constrained by external expectations of staying within one field of expertise throughout his career. He decided to embrace inner freedom by pursuing various courses and expanding his knowledge across different areas of interest without fear of judgment or failure. By doing so, David found fulfillment and purpose in his career.

Freedom from dependence on willpower and motivation is attainable through cultivating inner freedom and self-determination:

1. Understanding One's Values: clarifying personal values is essential for making choices aligned with one's true self rather than being swayed by external influences.

2. Embracing Authenticity: living in alignment with one's true values and beliefs allows individuals to make choices that resonate with their authentic selves.

3. Building Self-Confidence: developing self-confidence helps individuals trust in their abilities and make decisions based on what they truly desire rather than seeking validation from others.

4. Setting Personal Boundaries: establishing healthy boundaries allows individuals to prioritize their well-being and values, protecting their inner freedom and autonomy.

5. *Cultivating Internal Motivation:* focusing on intrinsic motivation fosters self-determination, encouraging individuals to pursue activities and goals that are personally meaningful.

Overcoming barriers and obstacles is possible through various strategies:

1. Lack of Clear Goals: setting specific, measurable, achievable, relevant, and time-bound (SMART) goals provides clarity of direction and purpose.

2. Overwhelming Tasks: breaking down overwhelming tasks into smaller manageable steps prevents procrastination by making the process more approachable.

3. Inconsistent Routines: establishing consistent routines provides structure and helps individuals stay focused on their priorities.

4. External Distractions: minimizing external distractions enhances focus and productivity; turning off notifications or creating a dedicated workspace can be helpful.

5. Negative Self-Talk: practicing positive self-talk involves replacing negative thoughts with affirmations that reinforce one's abilities and strengths.

6. Lack of Immediate Rewards: finding satisfaction in the process itself rather than relying solely on immediate rewards or external validation encourages perseverance.

7. Unrealistic Expectations: setting realistic expectations ensures that individuals do not become discouraged by setting unattainable standards for themselves.

8. Dependence on External Validation: shifting the focus from seeking validation from others to finding validation within oneself promotes inner freedom and autonomy.

9. Lack of Social Support: surrounding oneself with supportive individuals who uplift them can provide encouragement during challenging times; seeking out community groups or support networks can be beneficial as well.

By embracing the power of choice and taking responsibility for one's decisions, individuals can shape a life that truly reflects who they are and what they aspire to achieve. The journey towards inner freedom and self-determination may not always be easy, but it is worth it for the fulfillment and sense of purpose that awaits.

CHAPTER 8: MASTERING YOUR MINDSET

In this chapter, we will delve into the profound impact that negative thoughts can have on our emotions and our ability to live fulfilling lives. Negative thoughts often distort our perception of reality and hinder our personal growth. However, by understanding and managing these thoughts, we can transform our mindset and cultivate a more positive and resilient outlook.

The first step in managing negative thoughts is developing self-awareness and recognition. We must pay close attention to our thoughts and emotions, especially in situations that trigger negativity within us. By noticing patterns and recurring themes in our thinking, we can begin to identify the distorted or irrational thoughts that contribute to our negative emotions.

One effective way to identify and reassess these distorted thoughts is through journaling. By recording our thoughts and emotions in a systematic manner, we gain insight into the common cognitive distortions that may be influencing our mindset. For instance, if we frequently feel anxious before a presentation, jotting down the thoughts that arise during those moments allows us to analyze them for cognitive distortions such as all-or-nothing thinking or catastrophizing.

Once we have identified these cognitive distortions, it is crucial to challenge them by questioning their validity. We can ask ourselves what evidence supports or contradicts these thoughts; whether we are considering all the facts or fixating solely on the negative aspects; and if there might be a more balanced or realistic way to view the situation.

By examining the evidence objectively and considering alternative perspectives, we can start unraveling these distorted beliefs.

Reframing negative thoughts is another powerful technique for managing destructive thinking patterns. This involves replacing distorted thoughts with more balanced and rational ones—shifting from defeatist beliefs to ones of growth and possibility. For example, if we catch ourselves thinking "I always mess up presentations," reframing it as "I've had some challenging presentations but I've also done well in others—I am capable of preparing and improving," can help cultivate a more positive and realistic outlook.

Practicing mindfulness is an essential tool in managing negative thoughts. Mindfulness entails staying present and observing our thoughts without judgment. By engaging in techniques such as deep breathing, meditation, or mindful walking, we enhance our ability to stay grounded and focused on the present moment. Mindfulness allows us to become more aware of our thought patterns and less reactive to negative thoughts, ultimately reducing their impact on our emotions and overall well-being.

Seeking feedback and support from trusted friends, family members, or a therapist can also be highly beneficial in managing negative thoughts. By discussing our thoughts and feelings with others, we gain external perspectives that enable us to see things more clearly. Sometimes, others can spot cognitive distortions that we might overlook—providing valuable insights and support along the way.

Cognitive-Behavioral Therapy (CBT) offers structured techniques for identifying and challenging distorted thoughts. Working with a CBT therapist provides personalized strategies tailored to your specific needs. Techniques such as thought records—where you write down your negative thought along with evidence for and against it—and cognitive restructuring are commonly used in CBT to address negative thinking patterns effectively.

Setting realistic expectations is crucial when it comes to managing negative thoughts. Often, these distorted thoughts stem from unrealistic expectations that we place upon ourselves. By reassessing our goals and standards to ensure they are achievable and fair, we can reduce feelings of overwhelm while building confidence in ourselves. Breaking larger goals into smaller, manageable steps also helps us maintain a positive mindset as we make progress towards achieving them.

Practicing self-compassion is a fundamental aspect of managing negative thoughts effectively. Treating ourselves with kindness and understanding—especially during difficult times—reduces the impact of negativity on our mental well-being while fostering a more positive self-image. Acknowledging that everyone makes mistakes or experiences setbacks is an essential part of self-compassion. It allows us to embrace our imperfections and learn from them, ultimately leading to personal growth.

Real-Life Application:

To illustrate the power of managing negative thoughts, let's consider the example of John. He often found himself thinking, "I'm a failure because I didn't get that job." Recognizing this as a cognitive distortion involving overgeneralization and catastrophizing, he challenged the thought by asking himself, "What evidence do I have that I'm a failure? Have I succeeded in other areas of my life?" Through this process of questioning his thoughts and examining the evidence objectively, he reframed his belief to "I didn't get that job, but I've been successful in other aspects of my life. This experience is an opportunity for growth." By implementing these practices into his life, John successfully managed his negative thoughts and developed a more positive and resilient mindset.

Managing negative thoughts is a powerful tool for transforming our mindset and cultivating a more positive and resilient outlook on life. By recognizing, challenging, and reframing distorted thoughts; practicing mindfulness; seeking support when needed; setting realistic expectations; practicing self-compassion; and utilizing techniques from Cognitive-Behavioral Therapy (CBT), we can overcome negative thinking patterns. In doing so, we open ourselves up to embracing a more fulfilling and optimistic mindset. Remember: don't believe everything you think—take control of your mind instead!

CHAPTER 9: EMBRACING THE POWER OF MINDFULNESS FOR LASTING PEACE AND JOY

In our relentless pursuit of lasting peace and joy, we often overlook the transformative power of fully experiencing the present moment. The practice of mindfulness allows us to detach ourselves from past regrets and future anxieties, enabling a deep connection with the here and now. By cultivating a state of presence, we can reduce stress and anxiety, enhance emotional resilience, improve relationships, heighten awareness and appreciation, encourage acceptance, promote self-awareness and growth, increase productivity, foster gratitude, and break free from negative thought cycles. It is through the integration of mindfulness into our daily lives that we can discover unconditional peace and joy.

One of the most immediate benefits of living in the present moment is its ability to reduce stress and anxiety. When we constantly dwell on what might happen in the future or replay past mistakes in our minds, we miss out on finding solace in the current moment. Mindfulness helps calm our racing thoughts by redirecting our focus away from worries about what's to come or regrets about what's been. By gently guiding our attention back to the present moment time after time, we create space for tranquility to arise.

Moreover, being fully present allows us to experience and process our emotions as they emerge without suppression or avoidance. Rather than being swept away by them or pushing them aside hastily, mindfulness invites us to accept and understand our emotions in real-time. This practice enhances emotional resilience by fostering a healthier response to life's inevitable challenges. Accepting and acknowledging our emotions prevents them from building up unresolved within us – a buildup that can lead to long-term emotional distress.

Living in the present also has a profound impact on the quality of our relationships. When we are truly present with others – actively listening without judgment or distraction – it enables deeper connections rooted in genuine understanding. By offering this gift of presence during interactions with loved ones or even acquaintances, we create a space for authentic connection and belonging, ultimately contributing to our overall happiness.

Practicing mindfulness and being present heightens our awareness of the world around us, allowing us to notice and appreciate the small details that often go unnoticed. This heightened awareness brings a sense of wonder and gratitude for life's simple pleasures, leading to a deeper experience of joy. By savoring these moments fully – whether it's the warmth of sunlight on our skin or the delicate fragrance of blooming flowers – we can lead more fulfilling and enriched lives.

Additionally, being present encourages acceptance of the current moment just as it is, without judgment or resistance. This acceptance helps us let go of the need to control every aspect of our lives, leading to a profound sense of peace. When we accept things as they are instead of how we wish them to be, we reduce internal conflict and foster a state of inner calm.

The practice of mindfulness and living in the present moment enhances self-awareness by inviting us to better understand our thoughts, feelings, and behaviors. Through this increased self-awareness, personal growth becomes possible as we become more attuned with our true selves. By making choices aligned with our values and desires rather than reacting impulsively or unconsciously, we cultivate a more authentic and satisfying life.

Engaging fully in the present moment also increases productivity and effectiveness in all aspects of life. When we are fully focused on the task at hand – whether it's completing work assignments or engaging in leisure activities – our actions become more efficient and creative. This heightened focus not only helps us achieve goals more effectively but also reduces frustration that arises from being scattered or easily distracted.

Furthermore, experiencing the present moment fully promotes a deep sense of gratitude within us. Even during challenging times when everything seems bleak, there are usually aspects in life for which we can be grateful. Practicing gratitude shifts our attention from what is lacking towards what is present and positive, significantly enhancing our overall sense of well-being.

Finally, being present helps to break the cycle of negative thinking and rumination that often plagues our minds. When we cultivate a focus on the here and now, we are less likely to get caught up in repetitive, negative thought patterns. This shift in focus can alleviate feelings of depression and hopelessness, paving the way for a more positive and joyful mindset.

In summary, embracing the ability to fully experience the present moment is essential for finding unconditional peace and joy. By reducing stress and anxiety, enhancing emotional resilience, improving relationships, heightening awareness and appreciation, encouraging acceptance, promoting self-awareness and growth, increasing productivity, fostering gratitude, and breaking free from negative thought cycles – we can cultivate a deep sense of peace and joy in our lives. Through the integration of mindfulness into our daily lives – by gently bringing ourselves back to this moment time after time – we can find solace and fulfillment in each passing breath.

CHAPTER 10: TAPPING INTO THE POWER OF INTUITION FOR ENHANCED DECISION-MAKING AND PERSONAL GROWTH

Introduction

In this chapter, we will delve into the fascinating concept of intuition and explore how it goes beyond rational thinking to guide our life decisions. Intuition, often described as a "gut feeling" or an inner sense, is the ability to understand or know something immediately without conscious reasoning. It operates below our conscious awareness, drawing from a deep well of accumulated experiences, emotions, and unconscious information processing.

Understanding Intuition

Intuition is fast and automatic, providing insights or decisions almost instantaneously. It integrates multiple sources of information and experiences into a cohesive understanding without detailed analysis. These intuitive insights are often accompanied by a strong emotional response – a sense of certainty, comfort, or urgency. Additionally, intuition is context-sensitive; it is influenced by the specific situation and environment in which it occurs.

Comparing Intuition with Rational Thinking

Rational thinking involves deliberate logical analysis based on available data and evidence. While rational thinking plays an essential role in decision-making, it can sometimes be limiting – particularly in complex or ambiguous situations where not all variables can be quantified or when time is of the essence.

In contrast to rational thinking's slower-paced nature, intuition allows individuals to make quick and effective decisions when time is limited or when facing uncertainty. It guides interactions and decisions in personal relationships by helping individuals sense the underlying feelings and intentions of others. Furthermore, intuition plays a significant role in creativity and innovation – leading to breakthroughs that structured rational thinking alone may not achieve.

Enhancing Decision-Making through Trusting Intuition

Trusting intuition enhances decision-making by incorporating emotional and subconscious cues that rational analysis might overlook. It encourages individuals to listen to their inner voice and consider their true desires and values. This alignment with inner values can lead to greater fulfillment and success in the long run.

To develop deep intuition beyond what rational thinking can provide, individuals can practice mindfulness and mental presence. Mindfulness meditation, body scans, mindful observation, journaling, nature walks, and mindful breathing are all techniques that enhance awareness and attunement to intuitive insights. Visualization exercises, listening to the body's signals, and practicing patience also strengthen the intuitive connection.

Addressing Doubts and Skepticism

Addressing common doubts and skepticism about intuition is crucial. Many people view intuition as guessing or luck, but it is based on subconscious processing of past experiences and knowledge. While intuition is not infallible, it can complement rational analysis in decision-making. Intuition is a blend of emotional and cognitive processes – not purely subjective or mystical. Scientific research supports the existence and effectiveness of intuition.

Validating the Power of Intuition through Personal Stories

Personal experiences and stories of individuals who have developed deep intuition can inspire others to tap into their own intuitive wisdom. These stories demonstrate how intuition has led to positive life changes in various areas such as career shifts, health transformations, relationship decisions, and business success.

Intuition in Career Decision-Making

Intuition plays a significant role in guiding career decisions. When faced with choices regarding our professional paths – whether it's considering a new job offer or pursuing an entrepreneurial venture – rational thinking alone may not provide us with all the answers we need.

By tapping into our intuition during these moments of uncertainty or change, we allow ourselves to access deeper insights about what truly aligns with our passions and purpose. Intuition helps us consider factors beyond just financial gain or societal expectations; it encourages us to listen to our inner voice that knows what will bring us fulfillment in our professional lives.

Intuition in Health Transformations

Intuition also plays a vital role when making decisions related to our health journeys. In situations where medical diagnoses are unclear or treatment options seem overwhelming, relying solely on logical analysis may leave us feeling stuck or unsure about the best path forward.

By actively engaging with our intuition, we can tap into our inner wisdom and make choices that resonate with our bodies and overall well-being. Intuition allows us to consider not only the physical aspects of our health but also the emotional and spiritual dimensions that influence our overall wellness.

Intuition in Relationship Decision-Making

Navigating relationships can be challenging, especially when faced with important decisions such as committing to a long-term partnership or recognizing when it's time to let go. Rational thinking alone may not provide us with all the answers we seek in matters of the heart.

Intuition helps us tune into subtle cues and signals within ourselves and others, allowing us to make decisions based on a deeper understanding of what feels right for us. By trusting our intuition, we can navigate relationships authentically and align ourselves with partners who share our values, goals, and aspirations.

Intuition in Business Success

In the world of business, relying solely on rational thinking may limit one's ability to innovate or seize new opportunities. Intuition plays a crucial role in entrepreneurial success by guiding individuals toward unconventional ideas or strategies that rational analysis might overlook.

Many successful entrepreneurs credit their intuitive insights for breakthroughs that have propelled their businesses forward. By cultivating deep intuition and learning to trust it alongside rational analysis, individuals can unlock new realms of creativity and innovation within their professional endeavors.

Conclusion

Developing deep intuition beyond rational thinking is a valuable skill that can enhance decision-making, creativity, and overall well-being. By practicing mindfulness techniques, trusting inner guidance, addressing doubts and skepticism about intuition's validity, and embracing personal stories of those who have experienced positive changes through intuitive decision-making – we open ourselves up to tapping into our own intuitive wisdom.

Don't believe everything you think; instead, trust the intuitive insights that arise from within. The journey towards developing deep intuition is one that requires patience, self-reflection, openness to new possibilities – but the rewards are immeasurable. As we integrate the power of intuition into our lives, we gain a profound sense of alignment with our true selves, leading to greater fulfillment and success in all areas of life.

CHAPTER 11: NURTURING EMOTIONAL INTELLIGENCE FOR PERSONAL GROWTH

Emotional intelligence (EI) is a crucial skill that plays a significant role in our personal and professional lives. It involves the ability to recognize, understand, manage, and use our emotions effectively. In this chapter, we will delve into the significance of emotional intelligence, its core components, and practical strategies to develop and enhance this vital skill.

Understanding the Importance of Emotional Intelligence

Emotional intelligence is essential for achieving personal growth and success. It enables us to navigate social complexities, manage our behavior, and make decisions that yield positive outcomes. High emotional intelligence contributes to better mental health, improved communication skills, and stronger relationships. It helps us cope with stress, overcome challenges, and empathize with others on a deeper level – ultimately creating a more harmonious and fulfilling life.

Core Components of Emotional Intelligence

To develop emotional intelligence effectively, it is important to understand its core components:

1. **Self-Awareness**: This involves recognizing and understanding our own emotions, strengths, weaknesses, values, and motives. Self-awareness serves as the foundation of emotional intelligence by enabling us to see ourselves clearly and comprehend how our emotions impact our thoughts and behavior.

2. **Self-Regulation:** The ability to manage and control our emotions – especially during stressful situations – is key in developing emotional intelligence. Self-regulation entails staying calm under pressure while managing impulses appropriately.

3. **Motivation:** Emotional intelligence drives motivation by harnessing emotions to pursue goals with energy and persistence. Motivation stems from an internal desire for personal growth, achievement, fulfillment.

4. **Empathy:** Understanding others' feelings is an integral part of emotional intelligence known as empathy. It involves recognizing emotional cues from others while also understanding their perspectives in order to respond compassionately.

5. **Social Skills:** Effective interaction with others requires well-developed social skills such as communication abilities; conflict resolution techniques; teamwork proficiency; and leadership qualities.

Strategies for Developing Emotional Intelligence

Developing emotional intelligence requires intentional practice and self-reflection. Here are practical strategies to enhance each component of emotional intelligence:

1. Enhancing Self-Awareness

Mindfulness Meditation: Engage in mindfulness meditation to become more aware of your thoughts and emotions. Spend a few minutes each day observing your breath and noticing any feelings or thoughts that arise without judgment.
Journaling: Keep a daily journal to reflect on your emotions, reactions, and experiences. Writing down your thoughts helps you gain insights into your emotional patterns and triggers.
Seeking Feedback: Seek feedback from trusted friends, family, or colleagues about how they perceive your emotional responses. Constructive feedback can provide valuable perspectives on your behavior and areas for improvement.

2. Improving Self-Regulation

Breathing Techniques: Practice deep breathing exercises to calm your mind and regulate your emotions during stressful situations. Inhale deeply for four counts, hold for four counts, and exhale for four counts.
Pause and Reflect: Before reacting to a situation, take a moment to pause and reflect on your emotions. Ask yourself if your response aligns with your values and long-term goals.

Developing Healthy Coping Mechanisms: Identify healthy ways to cope with stress such as exercise, hobbies or talking to a supportive friend.

3. Cultivating Motivation

Setting Clear Goals: Define clear achievable goals that align with your values and passions. Break them down into smaller steps that are manageable – this will help maintain motivation while allowing you to track progress effectively.
Positive Affirmations: Use positive affirmations as reminders of past successes while reinforcing belief in abilities – this helps maintain a positive mindset essential for motivation.
Finding Your Why: Connect with the deeper purpose behind every goal you set; understanding why you want something provides intrinsic motivation which drives you forward.

4. Developing Empathy

Active Listening: Practice active listening by giving your full attention to others when they speak. Avoid interrupting and show genuine interest in their feelings and perspectives.
Perspective-Taking: Try to see situations from others' viewpoints. Ask yourself how they might be feeling and what they might be thinking.
Compassionate Responses: Respond to others with empathy and compassion. Validate their feelings and offer support without judgment.

5. Enhancing Social Skills

Effective Communication: Work on your communication skills by being clear, concise, and respectful in your interactions – both verbal and non-verbal.

Conflict Resolution: Learn to address conflicts constructively by focusing on finding mutually beneficial solutions. Stay calm, listen to all parties involved, and seek common ground.

Building Relationships: Invest time in building meaningful relationships, showing appreciation for others, offering help when needed, all of which contribute to creating a supportive network of connections.

Real-Life Applications

To illustrate the practical application of emotional intelligence, let's explore the story of Rachel – a manager who transformed her leadership style through emotional intelligence:

Rachel was known for her technical expertise but struggled with managing her team effectively. She often reacted impulsively during stressful situations, negatively impacting team morale and productivity. Recognizing the need for change, Rachel decided to work on her emotional intelligence.

By practicing mindfulness meditation and journaling regularly, Rachel became more aware of her emotional triggers. This newfound self-awareness allowed her to pause before reacting impulsively – helping her manage her emotions better. Setting clear goals provided motivation not just for herself but also for her team members.

Additionally, Rachel made a conscious effort to actively listen and empathize with her team members' concerns – fostering a more supportive environment while improving collaboration within the team. By developing effective communication skills and conflict resolution techniques she built stronger relationships that resulted in improved performance across the board.

Rachel's journey showcases how emotional intelligence can transform personal well-being while enhancing professional effectiveness as well as relationships. By developing and applying emotional intelligence, Rachel created a positive impact on her team and achieved greater success in her role.

Emotional intelligence is a powerful tool for personal growth, improved relationships, and professional success. By enhancing self-awareness, self-regulation, motivation, empathy, and social skills – we can navigate life's challenges with greater resilience and fulfillment.

The practical strategies provided in this chapter offer a roadmap for developing emotional intelligence effectively – allowing you to reap its many benefits. Remember that emotional intelligence is a skill that can be cultivated and refined over time. Embrace the practices discussed in this chapter while watching your emotional intelligence transform your life and relationships for the better.

As you continue on your journey of self-discovery and personal growth, don't forget to nurture your emotional intelligence – it will undoubtedly guide you towards a more fulfilling existence.

CHAPTER 12: EMBRACING CHANGE AND UNCERTAINTY

Change and uncertainty are inevitable aspects of life. Whether it's a career transition, a relationship shift, or an unexpected life event, how we respond to change significantly impacts our well-being and personal growth. In this chapter, we will explore strategies for embracing change and uncertainty with resilience and grace, turning these challenges into opportunities for growth and transformation.

The Nature of Change and Uncertainty

Change often brings a sense of discomfort and fear because it disrupts our familiar routines and challenges our sense of stability. Uncertainty, on the other hand, can create anxiety as we face the unknown. However, both change and uncertainty are integral to personal development. They push us out of our comfort zones, prompting us to adapt, learn, and grow.

The Psychological Impact of Change

Understanding the psychological impact of change can help us navigate it more effectively. Common reactions to change include fear and anxiety due to the unknown outcomes associated with it. Resistance may also arise as we cling to what is familiar because change threatens our comfort zone. Additionally, change often involves letting go of the past which can evoke feelings of loss and grief. On the flip side, positive changes can bring excitement and hope for new opportunities.

Strategies for Embracing Change And Uncertainty

1. Shift Your Mindset

Embrace a Growth Mindset: Adopting a growth mindset means viewing challenges as opportunities for learning rather than fearing failure.
Accept Impermanence: Recognize that change is a natural part of life; embracing impermanence helps us become more adaptable.

2. Cultivate Resilience

Build a Support System: Surround yourself with supportive friends who provide encouragement during times of change.
Practice Self-Care: Prioritize activities that nurture your physical, emotional, mental well-being.
Develop Problem-Solving Skills: Strengthen your ability to break challenges into manageable steps seeking creative solutions.

3. Embrace Uncertainty

Stay Present: Focus on the present moment rather than worrying about the future; mindfulness practices can help you stay centered.
Cultivate Curiosity: Approach uncertainty with curiosity and openness, seeing it as an adventure filled with possibilities.
Let Go of Control: Accept that you cannot control everything; adapt more easily to changing circumstances.

4. Develop Flexibility

Adaptability: Be willing to adapt your plans and expectations as circumstances change.
Reframe Challenges: Transform obstacles into stepping stones by changing your perspective.

5. Set Intentions

Define Your Values: Clarify your core values and use them as a guide when making decisions during change.
Set Realistic Goals: Break larger goals into smaller, manageable steps aligned with your values.

Real-Life Application

To illustrate the practical application of these strategies, let's explore the story of Alex, who faced a major career transition:

Alex had worked in the same industry for over a decade when he was unexpectedly laid off. Initially, he felt fear, anxiety, and grief. However, Alex decided to embrace the change as an opportunity for growth. He adopted a growth mindset and viewed the layoff as a chance to explore new career paths. Alex built a strong support system by reaching out to friends, family, and career mentors for guidance.

To stay resilient, Alex practiced self-care through regular exercise and meditation. He embraced uncertainty by focusing on the present moment and approaching his job search with curiosity. Alex developed flexibility by adapting his plans and exploring different industries and roles.

—

By setting intentions aligned with his values, Alex defined his career goals and pursued opportunities that resonated with his passions. Through resilience, adaptability, and a positive mindset, Alex successfully transitioned to a new career that brought him greater fulfillment and growth.

Embracing change is essential for personal growth and well-being. By shifting our mindset towards growth, cultivating resilience through support systems and self-care, embracing uncertainty with curiosity and mindfulness, developing flexibility, and setting intentions aligned with our values, we can navigate life's challenges with grace and transform them into opportunities for growth. These strategies provide a roadmap for embracing change and uncertainty, allowing us to thrive in an ever-changing world.

As you continue your journey of self-discovery and personal transformation, remember that change is a natural part of life. Embrace it with an open heart and a resilient spirit, and you will find strength, growth, and fulfillment in every new chapter of your life.

CHAPTER 13: INTEGRATING SPIRITUAL PRACTICES FOR HOLISTIC WELL-BEING

In the quest for mental freedom and personal growth, integrating spiritual practices can provide profound insights and a sense of connection to something greater than ourselves. Spirituality offers a holistic approach to well-being, addressing the mind, body, and soul. In this chapter, we will explore the benefits of incorporating spiritual practices into our daily lives and practical ways to cultivate a deeper spiritual connection.

The Role of Spirituality in Well-Being

Spirituality is the pursuit of a deeper understanding of life's purpose and our place in the universe. It is not confined to religious beliefs but encompasses a broad range of practices and experiences that foster a sense of inner peace, connection, and meaning. Spirituality can enhance well-being by providing meaning and purpose beyond material pursuits, promoting inner peace through practices such as meditation and prayer, enhancing compassion and empathy towards others, encouraging self-reflection for personal growth, and fostering resilience during challenging times.

1. Meditation

Meditation is a cornerstone of many spiritual traditions. It involves quieting the mind and focusing on the present moment. Regular meditation practice can reduce stress, increase self-awareness, and promote inner peace. Whether it's mindfulness meditation or loving-kindness meditation, find a practice that resonates with you and commit to it regularly.

2. Prayer

Prayer is a way of communicating with a higher power or expressing gratitude and intentions. It can provide comfort, guidance, and a sense of connection. Whether you follow a specific religious tradition or create your own form of prayer, make it a daily practice to foster spiritual growth.

3. Yoga

Yoga integrates physical movement with spirituality by combining physical postures (asanas), breath control (pranayama), and meditation (dhyana). It promotes holistic well-being by enhancing flexibility, strength, relaxation while fostering a deeper spiritual connection.

4. Mindfulness

Mindfulness involves being fully present in the moment without judgment. This practice can be incorporated into daily activities such as eating, walking, or even doing chores. Mindfulness helps cultivate a deeper awareness of your thoughts and emotions, promoting a sense of peace and clarity.

5. Gratitude Practice

Cultivating gratitude is a powerful spiritual practice that shifts your focus from what is lacking to what is abundant in your life. Keeping a gratitude journal, where you write down things you are thankful for each day, can enhance your sense of well-being and foster a positive outlook on life.

6. Nature Connection

Spending time in nature can be a deeply spiritual experience. Nature has a way of grounding us, providing a sense of peace and connection to the larger world. Whether it's taking walks in the park or sitting by a body of water, regular interaction with nature can nurture your spirit.

7. Reflective Writing

Journaling about your spiritual experiences, thoughts, and feelings can deepen your understanding of yourself and your spiritual journey. Reflective writing allows you to explore your beliefs, aspirations, and challenges while fostering personal and spiritual growth.

8. Community Involvement

Being part of a spiritual community provides support, inspiration, and a sense of belonging. Whether through religious congregations or meditation groups, engaging with like-minded individuals can enhance your spiritual journey.

Integrating Spiritual Practices into Daily Life

Incorporating spiritual practices into daily routines doesn't require drastic changes but small manageable steps that gradually build on each other:

Create sacred space: Designate an area in your home for meditation, prayer or reflection.
Set intentions: Begin each day by setting a spiritual intention or saying a prayer.
Practice regularly: Dedicate specific time every day for meditation, prayer or mindfulness.
Be present: Incorporate mindfulness into everyday activities.
Seek inspiration: Read spiritual texts, listen to uplifting music or attend spiritual talks and workshops.

Real-Life Applications

Consider the story of Julia, a high-stress executive who turned to spirituality for balance and fulfillment. Overwhelmed by her demanding job and constant stress, Julia decided to explore spiritual practices. She started with daily meditation, creating a calm space in her home. Additionally, she kept a gratitude journal, joined a local yoga class, and made it a point to spend time in nature every weekend.

These practices brought Julia a sense of peace and clarity. She became more present and mindful in her daily activities, leading to improved relationships and reduced stress. Julia's spiritual journey not only enhanced her personal well-being but also positively impacted her professional life, making her a more effective and compassionate leader.

Integrating spiritual practices into daily life can profoundly impact mental, emotional, and physical well-being. By incorporating meditation, prayer, mindfulness, gratitude practice, nature connection, reflective writing, and community involvement, you can cultivate a deeper spiritual connection and holistic sense of peace and fulfillment.

As you continue your journey of self-discovery and personal growth, remember that spirituality is a deeply personal experience.

Explore different practices, find what resonates with you, and make it part of your life. Embrace the transformative power of spirituality and watch as it brings greater meaning, purpose, and joy into your life.

CHAPTER 14: THE TRANSFORMATIVE POWER OF POSITIVE AFFIRMATIONS

Positive affirmations are a powerful tool that can reshape our mindset, boost self-esteem, and promote personal growth. By consciously choosing positive and empowering statements, we have the ability to transform our beliefs and attitudes, leading to a more fulfilling and successful life. In this chapter, we will explore the science behind positive affirmations, their numerous benefits, and practical ways to incorporate them into our daily routine.

Understanding Positive Affirmations

Positive affirmations are simple statements that challenge and overcome negative thoughts and self-sabotaging behaviors. They are based on the idea that our thoughts shape our reality. By replacing negative thoughts with positive ones, we can change our perceptions, behaviors, and outcomes.

The Science Behind Positive Affirmations

Research in psychology and neuroscience supports the effectiveness of positive affirmations. Studies have shown that affirmations can reduce stress by promoting a positive mindset while also boosting self-esteem and self-worth. Moreover, they have been found to enhance performance in various areas such as academics, sports, and work by increasing confidence and motivation. Additionally, positive affirmations can have a profound impact on physical health by reducing stress levels and promoting a positive outlook.

Benefits of Positive Affirmations

The benefits of incorporating positive affirmations into our lives are extensive:

Increased Self-Confidence: Positive affirmations help build self-confidence by reinforcing positive beliefs about ourselves.

Improved Mental Health: Regular use of affirmations can reduce anxiety, depression, and negative thinking patterns.

Enhanced Motivation: Affirmations serve as powerful motivators by focusing our minds on goals and aspirations.

Better Stress Management: By practicing positive affirmations regularly, we develop a calm and centered mindset which enables us to manage stress more effectively.

Greater Resilience: The use of affirmations builds resilience by fostering a growth mindset along with a positive attitude towards challenges.

Creating Effective Positive Affirmations

To ensure the effectiveness of our affirmations, we should follow these guidelines:

Be Positive: Frame affirmations in positive language. For example, instead of saying "I am not stressed," say "I am calm and relaxed."

Be Specific: Make affirmations specific to our goals and desires. For instance, say "I am confident in my ability to deliver a great presentation."

Use the Present Tense: Phrase affirmations as if they are already true. For example, say "I am successful" rather than "I will be successful."

Keep It Short and Simple: Make affirmations short and easy to remember for regular repetition.

Believe in Your Affirmations: Choose affirmations that resonate with us and feel authentic. The more belief we have in them, the more effective they will be.

Incorporating Affirmations into Our Daily Routine

There are several practical ways to incorporate positive affirmations into our daily lives:

1. Morning Routine: Start each day by reciting positive affirmations aloud or silently while getting ready for the day. This sets a positive tone for what lies ahead.

2. Visualization: Combine visualizing ourselves achieving our goals with repeating our chosen affirmations. By closing our eyes and imagining success while saying our affirming statements, we strengthen the connection between words and desired outcomes.

3. Affirmation Cards: Write our chosen affirmations on cards and place them where we can see them regularly – on mirrors, desks, or car dashboards – so that we can read them throughout the day as a powerful reminder.

4. Meditation: Incorporate affirmations into meditation practice by spending a few moments focusing on breathing before repeating chosen statements and reflecting on their meaning.

5. Before Bed Rituals: End each day with positive affirmation reflections where we repeat statements about ourselves and visualize future success before drifting off to sleep with a positive mindset.

Real-Life Application - Lisa's Story

Lisa's journey demonstrates the transformative power of positive affirmations. She struggled with self-doubt and negative thinking, which greatly affected her performance at work and overall happiness. Determined to make a change, Lisa incorporated positive affirmations into her daily routine. Standing in front of the mirror each morning, she repeated empowering statements such as "I am confident and capable" and "I am deserving of success." Lisa also visualized herself achieving her career goals.

Over time, Lisa experienced a significant shift in her mindset. She felt more confident, motivated, and resilient. Her performance at work improved dramatically as she began accomplishing her goals. Positive affirmations became an invaluable tool for Lisa, transforming her self-perception and leading to greater personal and professional success.

Positive affirmations are a simple yet powerful tool for transforming our mindset, boosting self-esteem, and promoting personal growth. By consciously choosing empowering statements and incorporating them into our daily routine, we can reshape our beliefs and attitudes with profound results. As we continue on our journey of self-discovery and personal transformation, let us embrace the power of positive affirmations. Believe in their potential to transform thoughts, behaviors, and outcomes – thereby creating the fulfilling life we desire through the power of our words.

CHAPTER 15: BUILDING A SUSTAINABLE SELF-CARE ROUTINE

Self-care is not just a luxury; it is a necessity for maintaining physical, emotional, and mental well-being. Taking intentional steps to nurture and care for ourselves is crucial in order to have the energy and resilience needed to face life's challenges. In this chapter, we will delve into the significance of self-care, explore its various dimensions, and provide practical strategies for establishing a sustainable self-care routine that can be incorporated into our daily lives.

The importance of self-care cannot be overstated when it comes to preventing burnout. By prioritizing self-care practices, we can maintain a sustainable pace in both our personal and professional lives. Regular self-care activities help prevent physical and emotional exhaustion by reducing stress levels through relaxation techniques and engaging in hobbies that promote calmness and well-being.

Engaging in specific self-care activities such as exercise, proper nutrition, adequate sleep, and regular medical check-ups enhances our physical health. These practices boost the functioning of our immune system while improving overall vitality.

Furthermore, self-care plays a significant role in improving our mental health by enhancing mental clarity, emotional stability, and overall well-being. Activities like meditation and journaling provide an outlet for processing emotions while promoting mental focus.

Taking time for self-care sends a powerful message - it shows that you value yourself. Engaging in regular self-care boosts your self-esteem by demonstrating that you prioritize your own needs alongside other responsibilities. Additionally, practicing self-care allows us to achieve a healthier work-life balance by setting boundaries between work-related commitments and personal life.

Self-care encompasses various dimensions that contribute to our overall well-being:

1. Physical Self-Care: This dimension focuses on activities that enhance physical health such as tailored exercise routines (e.g., walking or yoga) along with adopting balanced diets rich in fruits, vegetables whole grains & lean proteins.

2. Emotional Self-Care: This dimension emphasizes practices that help manage emotions effectively (e.g., journaling). Seeking therapy or confiding in trusted friends can also be beneficial when it comes to navigating complex emotional experiences.

3. Mental Self-Care: Activities stimulating intellectual curiosity (e.g., reading, learning new skills) and engaging in creative hobbies (e.g., painting, playing music) fall under this dimension.

4. Social Self-Care: This dimension emphasizes nurturing healthy relationships through social activities, spending time with loved ones, and seeking support when needed. Building meaningful connections and maintaining healthy boundaries are essential aspects of social self-care.

5. Spiritual Self-Care: Practices that nourish our souls by providing a sense of purpose and connection to something greater than ourselves fall under this dimension. Examples include meditation, prayer, or spending time in nature.

6. Practical Self-Care: Managing daily responsibilities effectively by organizing space, planning time efficiently & managing finances responsibly falls under this dimension.

Creating a sustainable self-care routine involves integrating self-care practices into our daily lives in a manageable and enjoyable way. Here are some practical strategies to help build a routine that works for you:

1. Assess Your Needs: Begin by assessing your current self-care practices to identify areas for improvement or areas that require more attention across different dimensions.

2.Set Realistic Goals: Set specific and achievable goals for incorporating self-care into your routine. Start small and gradually increase the time and effort dedicated to these activities. For instance, if you want to start exercising regularly, begin with short walks each day then gradually increase the duration or intensity over time.

3.Create a Schedule: Plan self-care activities strategically by incorporating them into your daily or weekly schedule as non-negotiable appointments with yourself - consistency is key when it comes to making self-care a habit.

4.Prioritize Self-Care: Recognize the significance of self-care in your life by setting boundaries & saying no to unnecessary commitments while making time for activities that nurture well-being.

___

5.Be Flexible: Life can be unpredictable; therefore be flexible with your routine allowing adjustments as needed without being too rigid - finding balance is crucial.

6.Practice Self-Compassion: Be kind to yourself as you implement your self-care routine. It is normal to face challenges and setbacks; therefore practice self-compassion and remind yourself that self-care is a journey rather than a destination.

Here are some practical self-care activities for each dimension:

Physical Self-Care:
1.Engage in regular physical activity like walking, yoga, or strength training.
2.Eat a balanced diet rich in fruits, vegetables, whole grains & lean proteins.
3.Aim for 7-9 hours of quality sleep each night.
4.Stay hydrated by drinking plenty of water throughout the day.

Emotional Self-Care:
1.Journaling: Write about your thoughts and feelings to process emotions and gain clarity.
2.Seek professional support through therapy to address emotional challenges.
3.Practice mindfulness or meditation to stay present and manage stress effectively.

Mental Self-Care:

1.Read books, articles or other materials that interest you.
2.Learn new skills or take up a new hobby to stimulate your mind.
3.Engage in creative pursuits such as painting, writing or playing music.

Social Self-Care:

1.Spend quality time with loved ones & build meaningful connections
2.Join support groups or communities that share your interests/experiences
3.Set healthy boundaries to protect your time & energy

Spiritual Self-Care:

Meditation: Practice meditation or mindfulness to connect with your inner self.
Spend time in nature allowing it recharge you while finding peace
Engage in practices that help you reflect on values and purpose

Practical Self-Care:

Keep living & workspace organized & clutter-free
Plan time efficiently balancing work, self-care & leisure activities
Create & stick to a budget reducing financial stress

Real-Life Application:

Let's consider Jake's story as an example of the transformative power of prioritizing self-care. At first, Jake was overwhelmed and stressed due to his busy professional life. He realized that he was neglecting his own well-being, which prompted him to make self-care a priority. Jake began by assessing his needs and setting realistic goals for himself. He created a schedule that included daily exercise, mindfulness meditation, and weekly social activities with friends.

Additionally, he made time for creative hobbies like painting and reading to stimulate his mind. Throughout this process, Jake practiced self-compassion and allowed himself to adjust his routine when necessary. Over time, he noticed significant improvements in his physical health, emotional stability, and overall happiness. His self-care routine became an integral part of his life as it enabled him to navigate challenges with greater resilience and well-being.

Building a sustainable self-care routine is crucial for maintaining holistic well-being. By prioritizing self-care across various dimensions such as physical, emotional, mental, social & spiritual aspects while managing practical responsibilities effectively; you can create a balanced & fulfilling life.

As you continue your journey of self-discovery and personal growth , remember that self-care is a lifelong practice . Be patient , compassionate ,and flexible with yourself as you build & maintain your self-care routine . Embrace the power of self-care & witness its transformative impact on your well-being & overall happiness.

By integrating the principles discussed throughout this book into your life , you will achieve lasting mental freedom , personal growth ,and fulfillment . Embrace this journey with an open heart & commitment to self-care ; you will discover the profound impact it can have on your well-being & overall happiness

CONCLUSION: EMBRACE YOUR JOURNEY OF SELF-DISCOVERY AND PERSONAL TRANSFORMATION

As we reach the conclusion of this book, it is important to reflect on the key principles and techniques discussed throughout the chapters. The journey of overcoming anxiety, self-doubt, and self-sabotage requires self-awareness, self-compassion, and the willingness to challenge negative thought patterns. By embracing these practices, we can tap into our intuition and inner wisdom, cultivate gratitude and positive focus, and learn to accept and let go.

The tools and exercises provided in this book serve as a roadmap for creating the life we desire. Mindfulness meditation, body scans, gratitude journaling, and journaling and reflection are just a few of the techniques that can guide us on this transformative journey. By consistently practicing these techniques, we can develop resilience and overcome common obstacles such as mind wandering and negative thought patterns.

To readers who are embarking on this journey of mental freedom, I offer the following message and encouragement:

Embrace Your Journey with Compassion
This journey is uniquely yours, and it is important to be kind and patient with yourself as you explore these new practices and principles. Growth and transformation take time, and every small step you take is a significant achievement. Treat yourself with the same compassion you would offer to a dear friend.

Trust Your Inner Wisdom

Within you lies a deep well of wisdom and intuition. Trust this inner guidance as you make decisions and navigate challenges. By practicing mindfulness and staying present, you will become more attuned to this inner voice and more confident in following its lead.

Be Open to Change

Change can be daunting, but it is also a natural and essential part of life. Embrace the changes that come with this journey, knowing that they are bringing you closer to the life you desire. Each challenge you face is an opportunity for growth and a step toward greater mental freedom.

Focus on the Present Moment

The present moment is where true peace and joy reside. By focusing on the here and now, you can release the weight of past regrets and future anxieties. Practice mindfulness in your daily life, savor the small joys, and find gratitude in the present. This practice will ground you and help you maintain a sense of tranquility and balance.

Cultivate Resilience

Life will inevitably bring challenges, but you have the strength and resilience to overcome them. Use the tools and techniques from this book to build your emotional resilience. Each time you rise after a fall, you become stronger and more equipped to handle future challenges.

Surround Yourself with Support

You are not alone on this journey. Seek support from friends, family, mentors, or support groups who understand and encourage your growth. Sharing your experiences and challenges with others can provide comfort, perspective, and motivation. Together, you can celebrate successes and navigate difficulties.

Live Authentically

As you gain mental freedom, strive to live authentically, true to your values and desires. Let go of societal expectations and external pressures that do not align with your true self. Embrace your uniqueness and pursue what genuinely brings you happiness and fulfillment. Living authentically will lead to a more satisfying and meaningful life.

Practice Gratitude

Gratitude is a powerful practice that can transform your outlook on life. Regularly reflect on the things you are grateful for, and let this positive focus infuse your daily experiences. Gratitude helps shift your perspective from what is lacking to what is abundant, fostering a sense of contentment and joy.

Continue Learning and Growing

This book provides a foundation, but your journey of self-discovery and growth is ongoing. Continue to seek out new knowledge, experiences, and practices that enhance your mental freedom. Stay curious and open to learning, and let your growth be a lifelong adventure.

I want to assure you that you have the power to create the life you desire. By embracing the principles and techniques in this book, you are taking proactive steps toward a more fulfilling and joyful existence. Trust in your ability to navigate this journey, and know that you are capable of achieving great things. Your commitment to mental freedom and personal growth is commendable, and it will lead you to a life filled with peace, joy, and purpose.

Embrace your journey with an open heart and a courageous spirit. The life you desire is within reach, and each step you take brings you closer to realizing your dreams.

Made in the USA
Columbia, SC
02 September 2024

41535438R00055